my secret

Craig C. Velez

First edition: June 2024

Library of Congress Control Number: 2024905761

Published by ccveepoetry Publishing
Instagram: @ccveepoetry
Facebook: CCVeePoetry

dedicated to

the most beautiful people
one could ever meet

we are one people
who should be celebrated
in one big gay book

Table of Contents

introduction

i am a lucky man
in all my years on this earth
i have been blessed
to meet good humans

purely fantastic
examples of folks
who just want to live
their honest authentic selves
such beacons of love

these pages contain
their most precious confessions
that live in my heart
eternally mine
to cherish and admire
and now share with you

i value their lives
they have enriched my spirit

i am truly blessed

all of their stories
enlightens the blind of us
if we dare let them
revealing aspects

of who we are as people

yes who we all are

my hope for readers
see yourself within this tome
allow yourself life
negative be gone
shake the tree of love and truth
enjoy its sweet fruit
as it nourishes
what it means to be human
understanding love

i love you my friends
i pray that i served justice
to your stories told

i pray these words reach
the eyes of those who need them
whoever they are

i can proudly say
without a reservation
i love all of you

yes...i even love *you*

my secret

dead to me

yes i was once dave
but he's dead and i'm brittany
this is my boyfriend
used to be holly
and now his name is randy

i'm she and he's he
together we're we

it shouldn't really matter

it makes sense to us

so there's no reason
to judge us with all the hate

our love is for us

the meeting

gran
        i have someone
i don't know how to say it

this is my girlfriend

                        i already knew
        i am proud of who you are

                beautiful freedom

        can you please tell me
        i always wanted to know
                this dark desire
        when with one like us
        together in the darkness
        the taste of her love

with green eyes i watch

your life is special
freedom to find who you are
to love who you will

with green eyes i watch
your young fluid ebb and flow
experimenting

aye discovering

looking at society
challenging the norms

find your special path
where you can be true to you
unlike what i chose

to the queer and neurodivergent

to those who are queer
to the neurodivergent
i am here for you

remember yourself
the specialness of yourself

simply amazing

no need to hide here

be who your genes preordained

without any shame

i will walk with you
hand-in-hand if you need it

i am one of you

to meadow

did i ever know michael
or only meadow
sashaying through life

did i even know the you
who did not know you
truly the same you
only with changed moniker
caterpillar like
unleashing beauty

discoverer of your truth
lady in waiting
blossoming flower

tracking like a hawk

tracking like a hawk
walking with hands clutched
swaying as they pass me by

curves and full roundness
sloping perfection

incarcerating senses

the wiggly walk
the chiseled features
electrifies the body

is it wrong
to feel this human burning
to desire both

first time

the first time i tried
when that warm silver magic
slid across taste buds
filling with wanting
more than anyone could give
yet would die trying

each lifeforce taken
deep into my burning core
past my beating heart
                          a fiery shot
subjugating my victim
as i drink it whole

                    it's not an illness

it's not an illness
not mental nor otherwise
nor am i confused
it's just who i am

rising delicate flower
unafraid to stare
hold my gaze upwards
flexing in the summer breeze
radiating hues

no reason to change
it would only harm myself
to be who i'm not

guilt

Is this love allowed?
Can something so beautiful
be condemned by God?

They say God is love
then why are we so hated
for how He made us?

Did the pastor lie
when he told us of our sin
or is he confused?

Why do I feel guilt
and confused about the love
promised by our God?

the word

why does he say that?
every time he passes by
telling me i'm gay

i already know
i don't need a reminder
from mister caveman

                    look at it this way
       from a different perspective
         one not filled with hate
            you should consider
            another motivation
             maybe he likes you

the choice

i have no idea
why i choose to stay around
this strangeling town

i have no partner
no options to even date
this town is too red

closeted bigots
who seek meat behind their wives
have become a drag

comfort is a cross
keeping me in this city
unready to leave

the news

the doctor told me
the reason i'm throwing up
pregnancy happens

mom and dad don't care
telling them flowed like honey
words too thick for them
i need to tell him
boyfriend not baby-daddy
that i still love him

what scares me the most
tossing my insides outside
losing my girlfriend

your son misses you

since you kicked me out
i found the love of my life
his name is cody
we have a nice house
our home is filled with respect
like you tried to teach
if you are willing
and able to be open
i wish you would meet

your feelings are clear
            i wish you didn't hate me

your son misses you

love so innocent

love so innocent
pale fingertips from far east
gingerly stroking
nut brown desi skin
as they nibble on their lunch

neither understands
what she really feels
basking in blissful touching

the room fades away
a blurry background
noise and light fading to gray
the moment focussed

letter to mother

my dearest mother

i only wanted a kiss
like you used to give
when i was a boy
alone and crying upstairs
when you held me tight

love suddenly stopped
flowing to your little boy
beavers dammed your heart
desiring love
i dared to kiss the concrete
below the rooftop

rainbow

the rainbow sings hope

i learned that when i was young
in religion class

God's sacred promise
after the great destruction
that we are all His

i feel that promise
everytime i see that flag
pridefully waving
constant reminder
of who we are as humans
of our hope and love

i am not alone

my 24th year
in magazines i forgot
revealed my idols
famous stars i loved
reporting that they were bi
what it meant to them

as those words held me
i understood a great truth
that in this big world
in its great vastness
the billions surrounding me
i
        am
                not
                        alone

after all these years

would you still be there
if i told you my dark truth
after all these years

you once told me yours
and i celebrated you
and your trust in me
i kept mine from you
not joining your bandwagon
always about you

it is time you knew
my taste is all inclusive
i have no limits

it is the person

your parts don't matter
how you were born means nothing
i want the inside

i can pleasure you
any way you need me to
like you can for me

it is the person
not the physicality
that i desire

i want you for you
passion can handle the rest
while we just be us

owning the moment

masculinity
seeps out of his suntanned skin
exciting my loins

his round mustached lip
calls out to mine freshly shaved
in locking embrace

chiseled from marble
his body belongs to me
my mud form is his

i count my blessings
my nails running down his back
owning the moment

<h1 style="text-align:center">ode to eddie</h1>

i love you eddie
no need to hide anymore
you are truly loved

23

we have lived our lives
do not take on our burden
false expectation
thief of hope and life
who leads us down such dark paths
our self destruction

rise up in vict'ry
smother yourself in freedom
wave your flag with pride

modern girl

bea had a career
a husband and three children
she's a modern girl

nancy loves annie
four dogs and seven acres
she's a modern girl

max has no limits
shares her bed with tom and sue
she's a modern girl

conform to yourself
live a life that's true to you
be a modern girl

born this way

the high heels i wore
when i was in the fifth grade
did not make me gay
            when i wore mom's dress
        that saturday in high school
                did not convert me
i already knew
when i kissed betty jo lee
girls were not for me
        i knew all along
        nobody influenced me
        i was born this way

deep in a red run city

cookie cutter house
cookie cutter street
deep in a red run city

no one suspected
no one ever knew
where the deviants held court

deep in a red run city

there wild parties raged
there their lewd guests played
hidden from nosey neighbors

deep in a red run city

fluids flowing free
friends free to be free
deep in a red run city

alterboy

bully alterboy
beat me up in the schoolyard
warm spring april day
till this very day
i still don't comprehend why
my twin would do that

we both sound like snakes
stolen playgirl mag hiding
in a backyard shed

back in middle school
he should have been my ally
why did he strike me

                    i'd rather be home

i'm over turkey
and all these crazy trimmings

pie brings me no joy
false smiles hurt my face
i know my family hates me
for loving my man

i'd rather be home
holding my husband in bed
cuddling cheek-to-cheek
our stubble scratching
my chosen fam'ly

my son is gay

oh my son is gay
i am so proud of that young man
happily married

his friends accept me
of course i accept my son
he's my pride and joy
i have only love
and his friends love who i am
we're all family
it's so beautiful
we can all learn from that group
love without limits

wedding night

wedding night in june
finally forced to perform
husbandly duties
somehow worried him

21 year old virgins
the newlyweds both

lips traced the midline
kissing lower and lower

just past the navel
he finally knew
his only true desire

her older brother

His love has limits

God forgive these thoughts
i want to sin with that boy
knotted human strands
pile of spaghetti
lost in sloppy messiness
drenched in thick sauces

mama forbids this
says it's a ticket to hell
written in some book

a book about love
telling me not to give in

His love has limits

the pics

let me get this right
your daughter received nude pics
full-frontal child porn
from her girlfriend beth

      should i break my sworn silence
          and tell this woman
            beth born sebastian
      has only male plumbing parts
           deceitful person

file with the police
they specialize in these things
help you find the truth

crushing in school sucks

it's extremely hard
yes, hard – that's the correct word
it's extremely hard
showering with them
after a hard fought ball game

well, mostly with him

he's so damned sexy

he doesn't know it
don't think he knows me

do i have a chance?
will anyone even care?

crushing in school sucks

he makes me feel pretty

he makes me feel pretty
i'm a strong alpha male
but when his skin rubs on mine
i melt into servitude
his will overtakes me
i am his barbie
factory-made just for him

he makes me feel pretty
walking hand-in-hand
with each of us holing a leash
our babies beside us

he makes me feel pretty
unpredictable text messages
awaken my dull thoughts
an alarm clock to reality
of the excitement that awaits us
in the bed
on the couch
on the patio

he makes me feel pretty
toothbrush dangling from his mouth
thick white foam falling
calling for me to clean him
those soft lips curled to speak
when only laughter escapes

he makes me feel pretty
when he tenderly kisses my forehead
signaling his departure to work
conveying through peck and heat
his undying need to be with me

he makes me feel pretty

he makes me feel pretty
coy wanton eyes follow his movements
and when he dances round the kitchen
i am compelled to caress his back
signaling my eagerness for dessert
that will be served steamy hot
away from the cooking fires

he makes me feel pretty
oh God he makes me feel pretty

he makes me feel pretty
when he holds my trembling body
soft lips tingle the back of my neck
security brought to my insecure soul
as he whispers those magic words

he makes me feel pretty

he will never know

he will never know
father would never get it
i'm not what he thinks
i'll never be him
taking a wife to my bed
sleeping with soft curves

i'm more like my mom
i dream of a protector
to hold me at night
to feel his scruffed cheeks
as we lovingly dance close

he will never know

straight and narrow

i am confuséd

define this straight and narrow
how does this apply?

how can a gay boy
who can't shower in public
because i'm obsessed
do anything straight?

there's no razor's edge for me
my pendulum hips
keep time with my steps
my feet leading the sashay

not straight not narrow

i dream of sparkle

my shoes are too tight
i breathe in sharp winded gasps
from their lack of style
this bland uniform
conforming to tradition
conservative "style"

i dream of sparkle
in a sea of black and brown
loafers and laces
and an eight by ten
photograph of my husband
holding our puppies

not allowed to feel

not allowed to feel
my meaningless emotions
only you matter

it's not important
i found the love of my life
who completes my soul
you sit there crying
about grandchildren not born
not celebrating
your pretty daughter
on the eve of her wedding
to her future wife

your little girl

i am not your son
your dream is not who i am
nor who i should be
i'm taking hormones
i'm growing into myself

my body transforms
ev'ry time I wake
into the womanly me
i was meant to be

do not forgive me
accept my sweet personage
as your little girl

my secret

i have a secret

something i want you to know
i am trusting you

fear and shame grip me
stonewalling my vocal cords

can i reveal it?
am i strong enough?
can i vomit the coarse words?
the dry heaving aches

here's my best attempt –
some of these previous words...
what you've read is me

skittles

take pause from your lunch
visit us in the lib'ry
join us for a spell
the bookhoard knows us
welcomes us every noon-time
calls us a coven

we have our own name
reflecting diversity
celebrating us
so if you're inclined
and want to join love and laughs
come meet the skittles